The Greeks

THE ANCIENT WORLD

The Greeks

Pamela Odijk

Silver Burdett Press

Acknowledgments

The author and publishers are grateful to the following for permission to reproduce copyright photographs and prints:

ANT/Fred Mercay p. 13 top; ANT/NHPA pp. 13 foot, 15, 16; Carol Barrie for the cover photograph; The Mansell Collection pp. 28, 33; Mary Evans Picture Library p. 19; Ron Sheridan's Photo-Library pp. 11, 14, 17, 20, 21, 22, 23, 25, 26, 27 34–35, 36, 37, 39, 40; Stock Photos pp. 12, 41; Werner Forman Archive p. 18.

While every care has been taken to trace and acknowledge copyright, the publishers tender their apologies for any accidental infringement where copyright has proved untraceable. They would be pleased to come to a suitable arrangement with the rightful owner in each case.

First published 1989 by
THE MACMILLAN COMPANY OF AUSTRALIA PTY LTD
107 Moray Street, South Melbourne 3205
6 Clarke Street, Crows Nest 2065

Adapted and first published in the United States in 1989 by Silver Burdett Press, Englewood Cliffs, N.J.

Library of Congress Cataloging-in-Publication Data

Odijk, Pamela, 1942–
    The Greeks / Pamela Odijk.
      p.   cm.—(The Ancient world)
    Includes index.
    Summary: Discusses the civilization of ancient Greece, including the hunting, medicine, clothing, religion, laws, legends, and recreation.
    1. Greece—Civilization—To 146 B.C.—Juvenile literature.
[1. Greece—Civilization—To 146 B.C.] I. Title. II. Series:
Odijk, Pamela, 1942–   Ancient world.
DF77.034 1989
938—dc20   89-33859
ISBN 0-382-09884-6   CIP
                        AC

Printed in Hong Kong

The Greeks

Contents

The Greeks: Timeline

7000 B.C.		6000			5000		400

Neolithic Age: settled agriculture began in the lands that were to become the Greek Empire.

Athens produced much
pottery at this time.

1000 B.C.		900			800

The first Olympic Games
were held in Olympia.

Classical Age: Greek lands extended. Greeks influence many neighboring cultures.

Athens was the greatest Greek city-state
at this time. The ruler being elected by the
majority of those allowed to vote (i.e.
Greek adult males) was introduced.

Alexander
the Great
was born.

Greece
at war with
Macedonia.

Alexander
the Great
died.

500 B.C.		450		400		350		30

Peloponnesian War:
this war was fought
between Athens and Sparta.

Alexander the Great crossed into Asia
Minor and captured Syria, Egypt, and
Afghanistan. He also went into India.
Aristotle established his school of
philosophy.

Developments in science and medicine.
Hippocrates established the Hippocratic Oath.
Socrates, the leading Greek philosopher,
lived during this time. Socrates
challenged all people to think and to
question much that was accepted as truth.

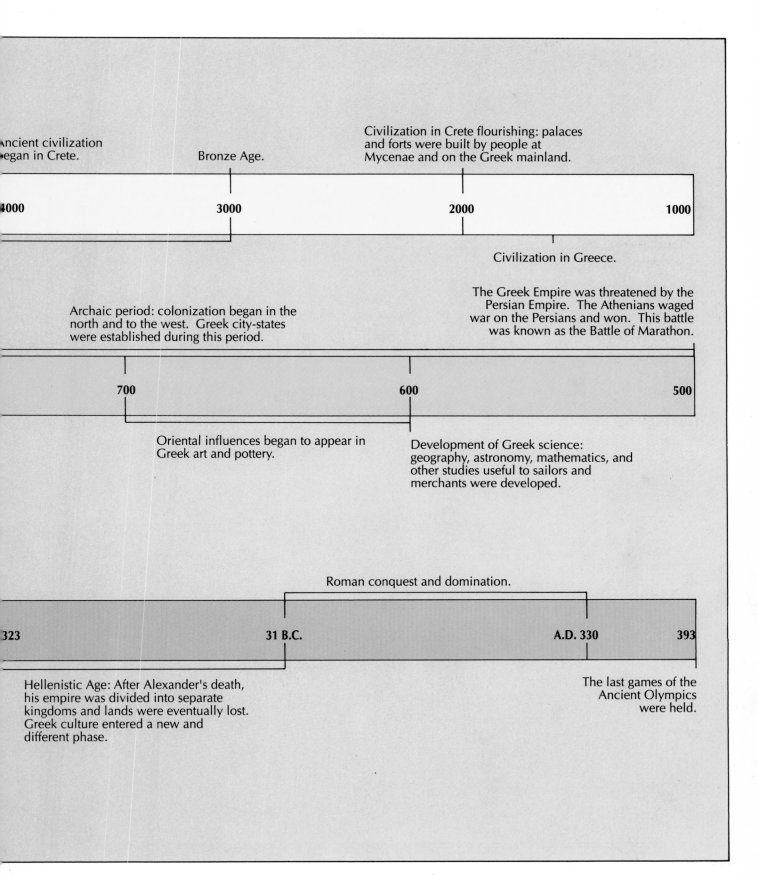

Ancient civilization began in Crete.

Bronze Age.

Civilization in Crete flourishing: palaces and forts were built by people at Mycenae and on the Greek mainland.

4000   3000   2000   1000

Civilization in Greece.

Archaic period: colonization began in the north and to the west. Greek city-states were established during this period.

The Greek Empire was threatened by the Persian Empire. The Athenians waged war on the Persians and won. This battle was known as the Battle of Marathon.

700   600   500

Oriental influences began to appear in Greek art and pottery.

Development of Greek science: geography, astronomy, mathematics, and other studies useful to sailors and merchants were developed.

Roman conquest and domination.

323   31 B.C.   A.D. 330   393

Hellenistic Age: After Alexander's death, his empire was divided into separate kingdoms and lands were eventually lost. Greek culture entered a new and different phase.

The last games of the Ancient Olympics were held.

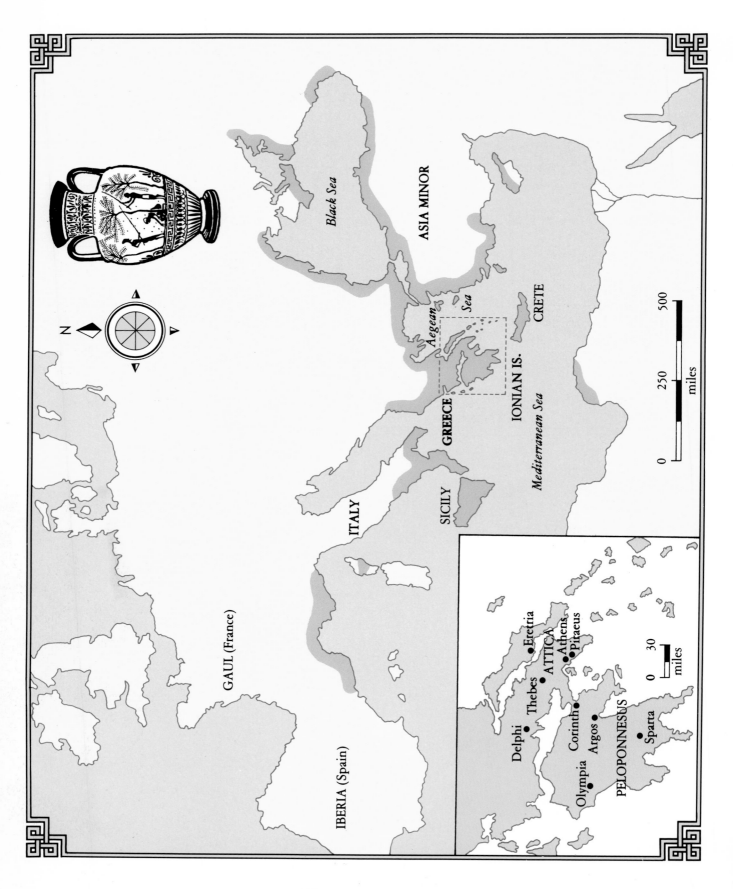

Black Sea

ASIA MINOR

Aegean Sea

CRETE

IONIAN IS.

GREECE

Mediterranean Sea

ITALY

SICILY

GAUL (France)

IBERIA (Spain)

N

500

250

0

miles

Eretria

Thebes

ATTICA

Athens

Piraeus

Delphi

Corinth

Olympia

Argos

Sparta

PELOPONNESUS

0   30

miles

The Greeks: Introduction

When we speak of the Greeks, we use a Latin word, *Graeco*, which means "Greek," the name given to the Greeks by the Romans. The Greeks called themselves Hellenes and their country Hellas and have done so since the sixth or seventh centuries B.C. The Greeks were very proud of being Greek and called all other people who were not Greek **barbarians.**

The history of Greece, meaning the time when Greeks exerted the most influence in the world, is dated from the first Olympic Games in 776 B.C.

In 776 B.C. the Greek world extended from Crete, in the south, to the Aegean Islands, and west from the coast of Asia Minor to the Ionian Islands. The Greeks ventured out to colonize many lands and, at its greatest, the Greek world covered the area (shaded) shown on the map at the left.

From 323 B.C. Greece entered a period called the Hellenistic Age. For another three hundred years the Greeks extended their influence not by wars and conquest but with new ideas and inventions.

The Greek attitude toward life differed from that of any other civilization. The Greeks tended to look at the whole of life, not just part of it, and devised systems to benefit everyone. They spent a great deal of time thinking about the purpose of life. It was from this new way of thinking that new ways of organizing and doing things emerged.

The Acropolis, Athens.

The period of Greek territorial greatness ended in the first century B.C. when the Romans, under the leadership of Emperor Augustus, organized most of old Greece as the province Achaea to be part of the Roman Empire. However, the Romans did not destroy the greatness of Greek intellectual and cultural achievements; instead the Romans adopted them. The Romans learned much from the Greeks and, in turn, passed on much of this knowledge. We owe much of our art, science, philosophy, music, dance, language, literature, and political and social systems to ideas and inventions that were originally Greek.

Greek history generally can be broken down into the following periods:

Name	When	What Happened
Neolithic Age	7000–3000 B.C.	Permanent settlements of agriculture began in the lands that were to become Greece.
Bronze Age	3000–1100 B.C.	Palaces were built in Crete; forts were built by people at Mycenae and on the Greek mainland.
Dark Age	1100–800 B.C.	Not very much is known about this time. The population declined and buildings were destroyed but it is not known why or by whom.
Archaic Period	800–500 B.C.	Colonization began in the west and north. City-states began. Greek civilization and culture began to influence others. 776 B.C.—first Olympic Games.
Classical Age	500–323 B.C.	Invaders driven out. Alexander the Great extended Greek lands and influence.
Hellenistic Age	323–31 B.C.	Alexander's empire was divided into separate kingdoms and lands and was eventually lost. Greek culture entered a new and different phase.
Roman conquest	31 B.C.–A.D. 330	Greece under the political power of Rome.

The Importance of Landforms and Climate

The landform and climate of any area determines to a large extent how the people live, what kinds of crops can be grown and where, and what kinds of animals can be raised and used.

Landforms

Mountains cover three-quarters of Greece. The highest is Mt. Olympus, rising to 9,550 feet (2,911 meters). Many peaks are over 6,000 feet (1,800 meters). Small valleys between these limestone mountains are quite isolated and difficult to reach, therefore providing the people in these valleys with some protection against invaders.

Mt. Olympus in Greece is 20 miles (33 kilometers) wide. This panorama shows the summit.

The coastline is rugged, with many inlets. The rest of Greece is made up of islands of varying sizes. The island of Crete is the largest. Some of these islands are suitable for growing crops. Many of the islands are covered with trees, but some are quite bare.

The limestone of the soil is porous, which means that water seeps through the soil very quickly. Since the mountains are high and the land area small, the rivers are short and small, and therefore, unsuitable for navigation and irrigation. Large deposits of sedimentary clays were used by the ancient Greeks in pottery, and sandstone was used for buildings and statues.

Travel by sea was often the easiest way of reaching another settlement or city. Settlements were surrounded either by mountains or sea, or both, with barely enough flat land on

The Island of Mykonos, Greece.

which to grow crops and raise animals. The fact that many Greek settlements and cities were separated by natural barriers helps to explain why many **city-states** developed in which individuals felt that they belonged to a city and not to a unified country.

Climate

The climate of Greece is Mediterranean, where the summers are long, hot, and dry, and the winters mild. In the mountain areas, though, summer temperatures are much cooler and the winters cold, with snowfalls. Rain falls during late autumn and winter.

Natural Plants, Animals, and Birds

Plants

Because the landforms and climate differed greatly from one area to another, the vegetation varied, too, from herb-like scrublands to oleander, bay, **evergreen**, oak, and olive trees to evergreen plants. Along the rivers, in the high mountains, and on the plains grew pine, plane, and poplar trees. To the north, oak, chestnut, and other **deciduous** trees grew. **Coniferous** forests, dominated by the Grecian fir tree, grew in the high areas. Black pine forests covered Mt. Olympus. There was plenty of wood for house and ship building.

Animals and Birds

In the forest areas lived wildcats, martins, brown bears, roe deer, and sometimes wolves, wild boar, and lynx. Here, too, lived animals that could adapt to dry seasons, such as jackals, wild goats, and porcupines. Birds included pelicans, storks, and herons, as well as many migratory birds, which came to Greece during the winter months. There were also many different reptiles and fish.

Storks (above right) and the jackal (below right) were some of the animals that lived in ancient Greece.

Crops, Herds, and Hunting

In the country Greek peasants worked small areas of land with primitive tools. Only about 20 percent of the land was suitable for farming. Farmers who could not afford land of their own often worked for a landlord. Often this was only seasonal work, such as helping at harvest time, after which farmers would be paid. If a farmer's family had no home to go to or if a farmer could not find another job in the country or the city, he was worse off than the slaves. The way the wealthy and the poor lived differed greatly and there were many poor peasant families. The nobility owned most of the land, which often included the best land. This use of the land encouraged the Greeks to establish colonies and trading routes. The Greek colonists planted seeds and raised animals sufficient for their needs and traded their surplus with the mainland.

Crops

The main crops were olives and grapes. Though olive trees grew wild in Greece, the Greeks learned how to cultivate them and to extract olive oil. Olive oil was used in cooking and was exported in large quantities to Egypt and other countries. Grapes, which the Greeks also learned to cultivate, were another main crop and were used to make wine. Wine was a common drink in ancient Greece and was exported in large quantities.

Opposite: olive grove in Corfu. Olives were one of the main crops of the ancient Greeks.
*Below: **mosaic** showing a lion hunt.*

So important were olives and grapes that the Greeks believed them to be gifts of the gods Dionysus and Athena, the son and daughter of Zeus, king of the gods.

Emmer (wheat), **lentils**, barley, and figs were also grown, along with small vegetable gardens.

Herds and Hunting

Pigs and sheep were raised for meat, and goats were kept for meat, milk, and cheese. There was not enough good grazing land to have large herds. Small herds of cattle, sheep, and goats grazed on any available hillside. The earliest known domesticated cattle were at Argissa and Nea Nikomedeia in Greece. Peasants hunted forest animals and birds for food and fished along the coast.

Trade

It was from the Greek colonies and from trade with other countries that the Greeks were eventually able to obtain sufficient food and other products. Grain was imported from the area of the Black Sea; textiles were brought from areas with sufficient space to graze sheep; silk was imported from China and came by way of Egypt; olive oil and honey were exported from Athens; fine wines from several of the Aegean Islands; and salt fish from the Black Sea and its rivers.

A wild boar leaping across a pond of water. Boar were hunted by the ancient Greeks.

How Families Lived

The Greek family unit was called the **oikos**, and was very important to the Greeks. In Greek families the man was regarded as the head of the house, and sons were given more privileges than daughters. Households included slaves and relatives, even though they might not all live in the same house. Children were usually born at home. Marriages were arranged by the girl's father, who also provided a **dowry**. Men usually married at the age of thirty, while girls were married between the ages of twelve and eighteen.

Men

Only men were citizens and could take part in government. Citizens over the age of eighteen spent their time at the Assembly or at the law courts, or if they were merchants, at the market place. When at home men were not expected to share the workload.

Shopkeepers and craftspeople worked regular hours. Peasants worked the farms as the seasons demanded.

Women

Greek women, especially Athenians, had a life of great responsibility but very little freedom. They were responsible for caring for the children; preparing and cooking all food; making, mending, and cleaning all clothing; and cleaning the house. Farmers' and shopkeepers' wives were also expected to help their husbands with their occupations even though men were not expected to share the work of the house. Slaves helped with most of these activities.

Sculpture of woman grilling meat.

Women were not permitted to leave the house alone, not even to visit friends or relatives. They were forbidden to go to the **gymnasium**, and rarely went to the theater. Religious functions and festivals seem to have been the only occasions when most women were able to have limited freedom and social contact. Some festivals were for women only.

Part of a Greek marble sarcophagus illustrating a shoemaker at work.

Not all Greek women were treated alike. In Sparta, which was a military society, women were highly honored. Girls were educated at home and received a very athletic education. They were taught to run, wrestle, and take part in athletic contests. Spartan women were expected to be strong and brave, and to give up everything in times of war. Though Spartan women had no political rights and did not serve as government officials, they were often asked for advice on important matters.

Children

Girls and boys were not treated equally, although each was educated in ways that would best equip them for their adult lives. The Greeks believed that education was important and that it involved more than simply attending school. Greek citizens believed that an education should enrich the mind and body, improve manners, and benefit the city-state. Usually, though, only boys went to school. From the ages of seven to fourteen, boys went to primary school, where they learned reading, writing, music, citizenship, and physical education. Each boy would be taken to school by a slave who would sit with the boy during his lessons and help him with his lessons after school. From the ages of fourteen to eighteen, boys could attend the gymnasium (high school), where they studied science, math, music, and public speaking. Education for Athenian boys usually prepared them to serve their city-state. For Spartan boys, an education prepared them as warriors. Girls could receive an education but usually were taught at home by their mothers rather than at school.

Slaves

Slavery was so much a part of the Greek way of life that it was never seriously questioned. Nearly all Greek citizens had one or more slaves. Slaves did most of the unpleasant and difficult jobs which the Greeks, themselves, would otherwise have had to do. Prisoners of war found their way into the slave markets. Also, children of poor parents and **foundlings** often ended up as slaves.

Victorian rendering of court amusements during the post-Alexandrian period.

Houses

Houses were built of **adobe** and built on stone foundations with earthen floors. Wood was used to build supports for verandahs, roofs, staircases, upper story floors, and rafters. Roofs were tiled. Sometimes slate, cement, or **pebble mosaics** were used to decorate the floor. Inside walls were painted or covered with plaster. Windows had shutters.

Farmhouses were surrounded by a wall to shelter and confine any animals.

Houses of the wealthy were larger but similarly designed, with gateways leading to orchards and gardens.

Houses were divided into women's quarters and men's quarters, even in smaller houses, and often husbands and wives had separate bedrooms. Guests in a house observed the same custom.

Furniture

Dining couches were the main items of furniture. Usually, the wealthy had many elaborate dining couches in their homes. Three-legged tables slid under the couches when not in use. Other furniture consisted of chests; cupboards; and chairs with curved backs and legs, and some with arms. Items were often hung from hooks on the walls. Quilts, curtains, and cushions were used.

The front door of a house was considered to be part of the furniture and belonged to the owner and not to the house.

The Greeks made use of tunnels and clay pipes to bring water from springs into cities. This water was piped to public fountains. Many houses had wells; some also had cisterns.

Ruins of ancient Greek houses on Delos.

Food and Medicine

Food and Meals

Greek meals consisted of meat, fish, fruit, and vegetables. Wheat and barley were ground to make bread or were made into a porridge. Most food was cooked in oil. Cheese also was eaten. The Greeks ate a great deal of fish, both fresh and dried. In later times a greater variety of food was available, which came to Greece on trading ships. The main meal of the day was in the mid-morning or in the mid-afternoon. Breakfast was usually very light and consisted of bread and fruit. Cooking was done over charcoal on an open fire hearth in the kitchen. Food was served on pottery platters or in pottery bowls. For the wealthy these bowls were beautifully ornamented. The poor people had to make do with plain pottery of lesser quality.

Formal meals were for men only. Men ate these meals while reclining on dining couches. Low tables near the couches were covered with food. Wine was served from a large bowl and ladled into cups. The tables were removed when the meal was over and water was brought in so that the diners could wash their hands. After washing the men would apply perfume, put garlands on their heads, make speeches, and drink toasts to the gods or be entertained by dancers.

Women did not recline to eat. They sat down to meals.

Medicine

Even though Asclepius was the god of medicine, the Greeks were the first of Western societies to separate medicine from magic and religion. Hippocrates, the son of a physician, was born around 460 B.C. and traveled widely in Greece and Asia Minor practicing and teaching. Hippocrates taught that "every disease has its own nature, and arises from external causes." Disease was not something that was sent as a punishment from the gods. By using his own powers of observation and reasoning he learned to diagnose.

A number of documents, called the Hippocratic Collection, have been found and are believed to be part of the medical library at Cos, where Hippocrates taught. Subjects covered in these documents include anatomy, clinical subjects, poisons, diseases of women and children, prognosis (predicting the course and outcome of a disease), treatment by diet and drugs, surgery, and **medical ethics**. The Greeks continued to be the guardians and teachers of medical knowledge after the Roman conquest.

Asclepius treating Archinos, fourth century B.C.

Clothes

The main dress in all periods was a linen or woolen tunic called the **chiton**. It was a cylindrical garment with seams up the sides and across the top with openings for the head and arms. Actors and priests wore chitons with sleeves. The length of this garment varied. Chitons of the women were wider than those worn by men and the two edges were brought together at the shoulder and fastened with a brooch. The waist was gathered in with a girdle.

A garment worn exclusively by women in the archaic and classical periods was the **peplos**, a large rectangular piece of woolen cloth folded vertically and worn several ways. The peplos was sometimes worn as a mantle, or cloak, which was called a **himation**. Women draped the himation over their heads when they walked outside the house, as did men and women in mourning. Statues show this garment being worn many ways. The peplos and the chiton became more and more similar over time.

Above: lion-headed bracelet, fourth–third century B.C.
*Opposite: **stele** of a young mother with her children shows the clothes worn by ancient Greeks.*

Changes in Greek Clothing

Historic Period	Trends in Clothing
Archaic (750–500 B.C.)	Overall patterns, ornamented fabrics. Men wore beards, which were often curled, and long hair.
Classical (500–323 B.C.)	Patterns restricted to borders and central stripes. Priestesses only wore white but other women used many different colors.
Hellenistic (323–30 B.C.)	Colors became more brilliant; violet was particularly popular. Servants and artisans wore dark colors. Men's beards, especially for combat, were shaved. Costly materials, such as cotton and silk, were worn as well as linen and wool.

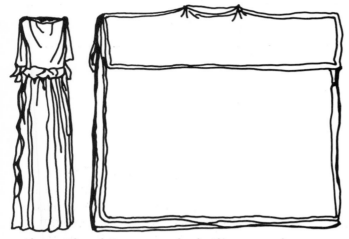

Above: the chiton, worn by both men and women, was a cylindrical garment sometimes made with sleeves, as shown on the right. It was joined at the shoulders, and gathered in at the waist with a girdle, as shown on the left.

Above: gold drop earring, fifth–fourth century B.C.

Jewelry

Jewelry created by Hellenistic goldsmiths was a work of art. Gold bracelets, **diadems**, and necklaces were made of gold that was hollow, filled with resin, and molded in the shape of acorns and rosettes. Greek jewelry resembled miniature sculptures.

Women wore their hair long, parted, and twisted into various styles. Young girls wore their hair plaited.

Both men and women wore sandals. Men occasionally wore leather boots and women sometimes wore soft closed shoes, especially during the Hellenistic period, when red and white ones were popular.

Children dressed in a modified version of adult costume, as children were regarded as miniature adults.

Left: gold disk showing the head of Athena, with interwoven chains, third–second century B.C.

Religion and Rituals of the Greeks

Pluto, ruler of Hades, the underworld, with Cerberus, the three-headed dog that guarded the gate to Hades.

Religion and Rituals

The Greeks worshiped many gods. They took their gods with them to other lands and often adopted the gods of the people to whose lands they went. Greek religion was always changing and evolving, especially during the time of Alexander the Great, when the Greek world was extended. There was no written creed or dogma, but sacred writings, such as hymns and lists of sacrifices to be made to the gods, have survived. Everything outside human control was attributed to the gods, who were believed to be immortal and all powerful.

After Death

The Greeks believed that the dead were led by Hermes to Hades, across the river Styx. Charon would ferry those who had received a burial. Coins for the ferryman were placed in the mouths of the dead. Supposedly, after judgment the people were sent either to Tartarus or to the Isles of the Blessed.

Temples

In early times caves or mountain tops were used as temples. In later times part of a king's palace would have an altar. Temples were built of wood but were replaced by marble later. Priests and priestesses were sometimes drawn from certain families; sometimes they were elected by popular vote. **Oracles** were taken very seriously.

Some Greek Gods

Name of god	About the god
Zeus	King of gods, also god of sky and thunder. Main ruling god of Olympus, weather god. Sacred animal—bull.
Athena	Patroness of Athens, goddess of courage, wisdom, and victory. Sacred animal—heifer.
Apollo	God of herders, the sun god.
Dionysus	A wine god. Sacred animal—panther.
Hades (or Pluto)	God of the underworld.
Hera	Goddess of marriage. Sacred animal—cow.
Demeter	A goddess of agriculture, harvest; corn goddess. Sacred animal—pig.
Hermes	God of science, commerce, eloquence, and cunning; messenger of the gods.
Aphrodite and Eros	Goddess and god of love.
Poseidon	God of the sea, god of horses, causer of earthquakes. Sacred animal—horse.
Hecate	Chief goddess presiding over magic and spells. Sacred animal—dog.
Ares	God of war.
Muses	Goddesses of the arts and sciences.
Asclepius	God of medicine.
Artemis	Goddess of wild animals, the hunt, and vegetation, and of chastity and childbirth. Sacred animal—deer.

Above: bronze statue of Athena.
Opposite: statue of Artemis, fifth century B.C.

Festivals

The Greeks had many festivals. One of the most elaborate was the **Panathenaea**, celebrated every fourth year at high summer. Sacrifices were offered, and the huge wooden image of Athena was provided with a new robe by the wives of Athens.

The Olympic Games, held for the first time in 776 B.C., were part of the great festival of Zeus. They were held every fourth summer. Truces were called during wars to allow the games to proceed. Only males participated. Females competed at the festival of Hera.

Obeying the Law

Because ancient Greece was organized into many city-states, each had its own political system and laws. Today we usually think of a nation as a political unit. In ancient Greece, each city-state was a separate political unit. Usually, the people of a city-state would feel that they belonged to that city-state rather than to the Greek world as a whole. Though each city-state operated independently, the people throughout Greece shared the same language and culture.

The Greeks believed that even though a society was made up of rich and poor, everyone should be treated similarly by the law, regardless of social status. The idea that everyone was equal in the eyes of the law was the beginning of **democracy.** Athens was one of the first city-states to have a democracy in which all male citizens had the right to participate in the making of laws.

Aristotle, who lived during the fourth century B.C. (384-322 B.C.).

Principles of Democracy

The Greek **philosopher** Aristotle listed the main characteristics of a democracy.

1. Every citizen could take part in government. In Athens, this meant that all citizens could take part in the Assembly and could be elected for a certain position.
2. Offices of government that are filled by election should be elected by the whole citizen body (in Athens, the Assembly), not by just a section of it.
3. The only offices to be filled by election in which only a section of the citizen body votes are those that need specialized knowledge or experience, like military command.
4. Offices are held on a brief tenure, which means that an elected person can only hold that position for a set short period, usually one year.
5. Sovereignty (supreme rule) rests with the whole Assembly, and not with the office holder.
6. Courts were selected from the whole Assembly body, especially for important cases. The Greeks did not distinguish between judge and jury.
7. Attendance in the Assembly and law court, and service in office are to be paid. What this meant was that all free male citizens were expected to participate in the life of their community. Slaves and women were excluded.

The Administration of Athenian Democracy

The administration of Athenian democracy wa organized in the following way.

Popular Assembly	All citizens could take part in the Assembly, which meant that all citizens could suggest new laws or changes to existing laws. The Assembly dealt with lawmaking and decisions of war and peace. It elected officials.
Council of 500	This Council of 500 assisted and advised the Assembly. It prepared matters for the Assembly. The Council was made up of citizens, chosen by lot.
Ten Generals	Ten citizens with military experience were elected by the Assembly each year. They became military and political leaders.

Laws

Laws were not uniform from one city-state to another. In the Athenian law courts there were no judges, only large juries. Usually 500 men made up a jury. Women were denied serving on a jury.

Laws were recorded on stone inscriptions and anyone was free to go and read them.

In Thessaly, women and men were equal before the law. In Sparta, Gortyn, and Crete, things were different again.

In Hellenistic times a new body of law evolved which became common law. Common law used carefully worded language and defined things clearly. Also in Hellenistic law, great importance was placed on written documents, such as those proving rights and obligations. Slaves were now also allowed to own property and take part in legal actions.

Some Aspects of Greek Law

Marriage There was no legal document. People were considered married if they set up house together, and divorced if one of the parties left. Under Athenian law a wife's dowry had to be returned if the marriage broke up. This requirement did give women some power.

Land People had the right to buy, sell, and lease land. Taxes were paid on land.

Property In Hellenistic law there was no real distinction between "ownership" and "possession" of "movable" and "immovable" property.

Inheritance An heir could inherit assets but not debts. Property was usually divided among all heirs. An heir could refuse an inheritance.

Maritime Law A **capitalist** would lend money for a marine expedition. Upon safe return of the ship, the capital and interest would be paid. Interest rates were high, 24 to 36 percent, because of the risks involved. This kind of transaction eventually developed into a type of marine insurance.

An amphitheater at Athens.

Greek City-States

The Greek civilization developed in many different places in Greece at about the same time. The oldest form of Greek civilization developed on the island of Crete about 4000 B.C. This civilization is known as the Minoan after King Minos. In about 1400 B.C. the Achaean people from mainland Greece invaded Crete and did much damage. Then, in about 1000 B.C. another branch of the Greek people, the Dorians, conquered the Achaeans and took over most of mainland Greece. The new invaders brought their own culture, language, and customs with them, and also absorbed some of the Achaean customs and culture. The Achaean people fled the mainland and went to the nearby islands. The area of the Aegean Sea became a mixture of languages, cultures, and customs of different branches of the Greek people.

Because the mountains and seas separated the people, each group set up a system of self-rule, and became a city-state. The city-states were not totally cut off from one another. People traveled across land and sea to keep in touch with each other. As such, all Greeks came to share elements of Greek civilization.

As the city-states grew, they needed more land for farms. Some city-states conquered neighboring lands to solve the problem, while others established colonies. From about 1100 B.C. on, the Greek way of living spread across the lands from the Black Sea to the Mediterranean Sea.

Because of the development of the city-states, each Greek had a strong loyalty to the particular city-state from which he or she came. But the Greek language, culture, and customs united the Greek people of different city-states. At the height of Greece's power, Athens and Sparta were two of the largest and most important city-states.

Greek Society

Greek society was organized along the following lines:

Citizens	Men could be citizens. Sons of citizens became citizens, and sometimes people who were either aliens or freed slaves were made citizens as a reward for doing something for the state. Citizens could own land and take part in government. Women could never become full citizens.
Aliens	Foreign-born people who were not slaves lived as free people but were not citizens. In Athens these people were called metics. Usually they were merchants, craftspeople, and artists. Metics could not own land or take part in government, though they were protected by the law. People who had been freed from slavery were in a similar class. In Sparta the equivalent class was the non-citizens. They were free people who lived in Sparta. Usually they were farmers, craftspeople, and traders.
Slaves	Slaves were people who had been captured and brought to Greece from other regions, though some poor Greeks were put into slavery. Slaves did most of the work. Most citizens owned slaves. In Sparta the slave population was larger than the other classes. The possibility of a slave revolt may be one of the reasons why the Spartans were always ready for war.

Writing It Down: Recording Things

Alphabet

The Greek language itself can be traced from the fourteenth century B.C., but it was not until the eighth century B.C. that the Greeks adopted the Phoenician alphabet of northwest Syria and adapted it for their own use. The major change made by the Greeks to this alphabet was the invention of five letters to represent vowel sounds. Not all Greeks adapted the alphabet in the same way and the form differed from one city to another. By the fourth century B.C., the alphabet became uniform throughout the Greek world. This alphabet served as a model for later alphabets, including the one we use today.

The Greeks wrote on **papyrus** rolls that were obtained from Egypt through the port of Byblos in modern Lebanon. Our word *bible* comes from Byblos.

The opportunity to learn to read and write was available to all Greeks from the sixth century B.C. onward.

Written Law

Public laws and other important information such as accounts and inventories were inscribed in stone and placed where everyone could read them and make copies.

Shorthand

The Greek historian Xenophon used an ancient Greek system of shorthand to write his recollections of the philosopher Socrates.

Mathematics

Greek mathematics were well developed by the second half of the fifth century B.C. Numerals were devised for the numbers one to nine, and various symbols denoted the number ten. A notation system was devised.

π = pi = 5	△ delta = 10
H = Hekaton = 100	× = chi = 1,000
M = Mu = 10,000	

Greek mathematics devoted itself to abstract thinking and calculation, and gave rise to advances in **geometry**. **Trigonometry** was also used in astronomy.

The Greek astronomer Aristarchus of Samos, in the third century B.C., first put forward the theory that the sun was the center of the universe and not the earth.

The ancient Greek alphabet, circa 450 B.C.

31

Euclid, a famous Greek mathematician.

Weights and Measures

The basic Greek unit was a finger, which was equal to ¾ inch (19.3 mm).

    16 fingers = 1 foot (30.8 centimeter)
    24 fingers = 1½ feet (1 Olympic cubit)

Liquids were measured in metrétés.
A metrété was equal to 7 pints (39.4 liters). The basic Greek unit of weight was a talent, which was equal to 57 pounds (25.8 kilogram).
    The Romans later adopted the Greek system of weights and measures.

The Calendar

Every city-state had its own method of recording time. The city-states also had different names for the months and the New Year, which began at different times, even though each tried to keep the calendar in rhythm with the seasons. In classical times the months began with the new moon and were named after festivals in each city.
    The names of Athenian months follow:

    Hekatombaion (mid-summer)
    Metageitnion
    Boedromion
    Pyanopsion
    Maimakterion
    Poseidon
    Gamelion
    Anthesterion
    Elaphebolion
    Mounychion
    Thargelion
    Skirophorion

After Alexander the Great's conquests, other calendars were adopted by the Greeks but some city-states kept their own calendars until about A.D. 200.
    To recall events, Greeks would refer to local magistrates or kings, such as "when Pleistolas was **ephor**," or from lists of victors at the Olympic Games.

Other Famous Greek Mathematicians and Scientists

Euclid was a mathematician whose great work in geometry was called *Elements*.

Archimedes discovered **specific gravity**.

Eratosthenes estimated the diameter of the earth to within a few hundred miles.

Hipparchus calculated the **equinoxes**.

Pythagoras contributed to mathematics, philosophy, and music.

Greek Legends and Literature

Greek Legends

The Greeks had a great love of stories and tales. These stories included myths and legends about the gods and the universe, and were told in a way that made these things understandable to the people. The Greek legends told of heroes, heroines, and events in ways that were part truth and part fiction. The Greek myths found their way into the arts and literature of the Western world. Scientists have retained the practice of naming stars and planets after Greek gods and heroes.

Homer

The poems of Homer, the *Iliad* and the *Odyssey*, are the oldest literary source of Greek myth and legend. Homer arranged many of the myths of the gods in an entertaining way. He assembled the gods on Mt. Olympus and detailed their activities, loves, and hates. Hesiod also wrote about the origin of the gods and told the tales of Zeus and Pandora, who opened an urn and released evil into the world.

Other Important Works

Other important works include the writings of the following individuals:

1. Aristophanes—who was the greatest representative of Greek comedy;

2. Xenophon, Pindar, Archilonchus, Sappho, and Menander—poets and dramatists;

3. Aeschylus, Sophocles, and Euripides—who wrote plays about a variety of subjects in the fifth century B.C.;

4. Callimachus—poet from the third century B.C. who recorded some of the lesser myths;

5. Euhemerus—who wrote about the early life of the gods as humans;

6. Apollonius—who wrote in the third century B.C. about Jason and the Argonauts; and

Stone relief illustrating a scene from Homer's classic tale of Ulysses, with sirens.

7. Herodotus—"the father of history"—active in the second half of the fifth century B.C.

Legends

Greek legends are stories of heroes and heroines who actually lived and include tales of the Trojan War, the Sack of Troy, the work of Heracles, and the legend of the Minotaur. These legends glorified the people and places involved.

Folk Tales

These stories were told simply to entertain and many had similar themes.

1. Odysseus—one of the Greek leaders in the siege of Troy who had many adventures on his way home to Ithaca.

2. Orpheus, Heracles, Odysseus, and Theseus—about journeys into the land of the dead; and

3. Perseus, Cadmus, Pelops, and Oedipus—about the victory of a person against great odds.

Art and Architecture

In Greece, art and architecture belonged to the people. Classical Greece was almost completely without palaces or private mansions. The system of government that made laws concerning taxes also provided for the construction and maintenance of public buildings and temples. Art was a part of daily life and not only for the enjoyment of the wealthy or for those with leisure time. Art abounded in theaters, temples, and cemeteries, as well as in private homes, where many everyday objects were beautiful in design and decoration.

Architecture and Sculpture

Religious architecture was very important in ancient Greece. It attracted many leading artists, including the sculptor Phidias, who constructed a huge statue of Athena for the Parthenon, an image of Zeus for a temple at Olympia, and another bronze statue of Athena for the Acropolis. Since athletics were part of religious festivals, statues of victors and ideal heroes and heroines were created. Heroes were usually shown nude. After the fifth cen-

Stele of Timarista from island of Rhodes, fifth century B.C.

tury B.C. politicians, orators, writers, and philosophers were also honored with statues. Color was applied to Greek statues. Later the Romans made copies of Greek statues.

One of the most famous Greek architects was Ictinus (or Iktinos), from the fifth century B.C., who was known for his work on the Parthenon at Athens, the Temple of the Mysteries at Eleusis, the Temple of Apollo Epicurius at Bassae, and other buildings. He was a friendly rival of the architect Callicrates (or Kallikrates), who designed the Temple of Athena Nike on the Athenian Acropolis and cooperated with Ictinus on the Parthenon.

Painting and Pottery

From the early bronze age, well-shaped painted pottery was produced in Greece. By the year 1000 B.C., Athens was one of the leading cities in the development of this art. Most objects were functional as well as beautiful. Two techniques called **red figured** and an earlier **black figured** were used. Many fine examples are preserved today. The gigantic **amphoras** and **kraters** served as funeral monuments. The figure painting on Greek vases established a tradition lasting until the end of the classical period. By the fourth century, painted figurative pottery became less popular.

Instead, the painting of **murals**, first in public buildings and later in royal palaces, occupied artists. The most famous of Greek painters was Apelles, who was Alexander's court painter.

Greek amphitheater at Delphi.

Music, Dancing, and Recreation

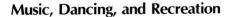

Music, Dancing, and Recreation

Although very little Greek music actually has survived, music and dancing were regarded by the Greeks as essential elements in developing the mind as well as the body. The Greek education system emphasized music and gymnastics.

The philosophers Plato and Aristotle believed that music had a direct influence upon the souls and actions of people. Plato demanded a place for dance in his ideal republic. Socrates supported the Spartan custom of teaching boys to dance, claiming that the best dancers made the best warriors. Flute players were also aboard Greek ships to keep the rowers in time.

Everyone was taught to sing and play musical instruments. Instruments included the flute, lyre, trumpets, and **aulos**. Drums, traditionally a woman's instrument in the East, were introduced in the sixth century B.C.

Music and dance came together in Greek theater where many kinds of dances were performed. Early Greek drama was tied closely to religion, but in the Hellenistic period, theater lost this religious sense. Greek auditoriums holding from 10,000 to 20,000 people were built. Performances were held in the open air. Simple stage props were used with painted scenes, but actors' costumes were very elaborate.

We have very little information about actual Greek dances, but vase paintings show dances being performed. The writing of dance steps was originally called *choregraphie*, from the Greek *choreia*, which means "dance," and *graphien*, which means "write." Our word **choreography** comes from this.

Musicians playing lyre and flute, 450 B.C.

Invention of the Organ

A Greek engineer, Ctesibius, living in Alexandria, Egypt, in the third century B.C., is credited with inventing the organ. His instrument used a piston pump to supply air through a valve to a wind chest.

Pythagoras, the Greek mathematician, added music to his studies and laid the foundation for the study of **acoustics** by discovering the relationship between the pitch of a note and the length of a string. Later, Aristoxenus was the main historian and theoretician of Greek music.

Going Places: Transportation, Exploration, and Communication

On Land

In a mountainous country like Greece, the easiest mode of transportation was on foot. Porters were used to help carry luggage for those who could afford to pay. Pack animals, such as mules and donkeys, and ox-drawn carts were also used. Greek roads were almost nonexistent. Heavy loads, such as large blocks of stone, were transported by animals. Inscriptions tell of hauling teams of twenty or thirty oxen, but these were rare.

The Greeks turned to ships as most places could be reached quite easily by sea. The lack of good farming land sent the Greek explorers to new areas in search of food and other products.

Maps and Geography

In the ancient world the Greeks were outstanding in their pursuit of geographic knowledge. Miletus, the Greek city in the east, became a center for geographic knowledge in about 600 B.C. Hecateus, a scholar from Miletus, produced the first book on geography in about 500 B.C. Later, between 27 B.C. and A.D. 14, the Greek geographer and historian Strabo wrote about many things. Herodotus, the Greek historian, also had an interest in geography.

The Sea

The Greeks had a shortage of good farming land and an abundant supply of timber to build ships. Their ships were of two kinds, warships and trading ships. Their ships adopted many features from the Egyptians.

Trading Ships

There were no regular sailings, and winter sailings were avoided. Piracy was common so trading ships were often protected by warships. The wide-beamed trading ships were powered by sail. They made their way from Athens to the Black Sea, carrying wine and olives in pottery amphoras, and timber to be traded for grain, hides, wool, copper, gold, glass, and other commodities.

We read of Pytheas of Massalia circumnavigating Britain and reaching Jutland (Norway). Trade journeys were made by land and sea to India to obtain spices, ivory, and **frankincense.**

Colonies

In the eighth, seventh, and sixth centuries B.C. many colonies were established in various parts of the Mediterranean by the old Greek cities. In most cases the need was for more farmland, but trade was also important. The earliest colonies were founded in Sicily and southern Italy. Many followed in the Black Sea and the northern Aegean, a few in the South of France and North Africa. In later years, Alexander the Great expanded the Greek world to include all of the former Persian Empire from Egypt to Afghanistan to India. Greeks also lived in Egypt, Syria, and Asia Minor. The cities of Alexandria, Antioch, and Pergamum became great centers of trade and education.

Detail of Grecian warship and cargo ship, 500 B.C.

Wars and Battles

Battle Dress

In the archaic period the army was composed of heavily armored **hoplites**, who were ordinary citizens trained to fight in close formation. Horses were few, as **cavalry** was not suited to the mountainous areas and horses were expensive. Each hoplite wore armor of beaten bronze which the soldier, himself, had to supply. His wood and bronze shield was most important. It was designed to be held either by a bronze handle or a leather thong so the soldier could have both hands free and not lose his shield. He wore a bronze helmet lined with fabric that covered the whole head. The body was protected by armor made either from sheet bronze or from linen to which many bronze scales were sewn. This garment was called a **cuirass**. Along with it went shoulder, ankle, and thigh guards.

Weapons

Bows and arrows were used but these had a limited range. Far more effective was the **catapult**, which could hurl stones a long distance. In later years Alexander's army made great use of catapults. Round stone cannon balls weighing from 15 to 88 pounds (7 to 40 kilograms) have been found near ancient Greek war sites. These findings suggest that large catapults were hidden inside towers to keep invaders' catapults out of range.

Spartans

Sparta kept a regular army in which all men were trained from an early age. Even upon marriage, at about twenty years of age, Spartan men had to remain at the regimental barracks for another ten years. Sparta needed a strong army to control the large number of semi-slaves, called **helots**, who produced all the food. The Spartans always feared a slave rebellion.

Fighting Ships

Fighting ships, or galleys, were called **uniremes**. These ships had, besides a sail, a single bank of oars and curved stems and sterns. The oars were used to power the ship, instead of the sail, if required. These uniremes later gave way to the larger **biremes**, which had two banks of oars and resembled the Phoenician ships in many ways. Later came the even larger **triremes**, with three banks of oars (eighty-five on each side). The triremes became the main Greek fighting ship in later times. The mast could be lowered and stowed away for battle. Later a ram was fitted to split or capsize enemy vessels. A platform called a storming bridge was added to make it easier for the crew to board an enemy ship. The captains of triremes were wealthy men appointed by the State to fit out and operate a ship for a year.

Ships were navigated by experienced seamen. The crew consisted of about 200 officers and heavily armed marines called **epibatai**, who were paid a **drachma** a day. To deter deserters, half of this money was withheld until the ship returned. Slaves generally were not used on Greek warships. Fighting ships had little room for provisions, so they could not remain at sea for very long.

In later times came the **quadremes** and **quinqueremes**.

Warriors in battle.

Famous Wars and Battles

Greco-Persian Wars (546—448 B.C.)	Fought on and off for about 100 years. The Greeks eventually won, thus preserving the liberty of the Greek states and keeping the Persians out of the Aegean Sea.
Great Peloponnesian War (431—404 B.C.)	This war was fought between Sparta and Athens.

Famous battles against the Persians:

Battle of Marathon	490 B.C.
Battle of Thermopylae	480 B.C.
Battle of Salamis	480 B.C.

Alexander the Great's Campaigns (336–323 B.C.)

Alexander was the son of Philip II of Macedon, which was the leading state in ancient Greece. Philip of Macedon intended to become master of Greece but was **assassinated.** Alexander took his place and finally became ruler of Macedon, Greece, Western Asia, and Egypt. He spent his life from the age of twenty until his death at the age of thirty-three entirely in military campaigns. As a result of Alexander's successful campaigns, Greek kingdoms were established as far east as India. Camels and elephants were used in Alexander's march of 4,000 miles from Egypt through Persia to India.

Greek Inventions and Special Skills

Democratic Government

The Greeks were the first to believe that people should have some say in making the laws that they were expected to obey. In other cultures, nobles, aristocrats, or priests made laws for the ordinary people, so the Greek way was quite different. However, scholars argue that we should think carefully about the Greek form being a true democracy because non-Greeks, women, and slaves were not given a say in the proceedings, yet were expected to obey the laws. The Greek way did establish a form of government that has survived, although with adjustments and differences. The opposite form of government is a **dictatorship** (absolute rule by a king, queen, or other ruler).

Other Discoveries

Greek discoveries in medicine, mathematics, science, music, art, geography, and architecture have already been mentioned but several lesser achievements originated in Greece. They include:

Machines for grinding fine flour and cereals. The first were circular mills with large grinding stones turned by donkeys. In the Hellenistic period a more efficient water mill was invented.

Perspective drawing was part of Greek art and architecture. It involved drawing a building or the human body from any angle and placing things in a sensible relationship with each other so they resembled reality.

Clocks were originally water operated but included a driving mechanism that indicated hours on a dial.

Gold medallion from Macedonia, third century B.C.

Greek Philosophy

Philosophers try to understand the world. Before the Greek philosophers, people tended to create myths to explain things that they did not understand. The Greeks attempted to find explanations for the origin of the world and the universe. The philosophy of attempting to find rational explanations is one we adopt today, and is used to make scientific discoveries.

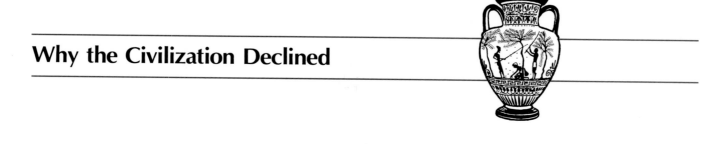

Why the Civilization Declined

Because so much from the civilization of ancient Greece has survived to modern times, it would be wrong to say that the Greek civilization declined. Greek territories that had been conquered by Alexander the Great and made part of Greece were gradually lost and, eventually, Greece came under the political control of Rome by 31 B.C. Other countries subsequently controlled Greece.

Because the Greeks were advanced in numerous fields, the Romans knew that adopting Greek traditions would be to their advantage. Most doctors, artists, lawyers, and other professionals in Roman times were Greek.

The Greeks might have been conquered in a military sense, but eventually, the Greeks outlasted their conquerors in an intellectual and cultural sense. The Greek civilization did not really decline.

Below and left: modern-day descendants of the ancient Greeks.

Glossary

Acoustics The science and study of sound.

Adobe Sun-dried brick. Used in countries that have a low rainfall.

Amphora A clay pot with two handles on the neck, used for storing and transporting liquids such as wine and olive oil.

Assassinate To murder for political reasons, such as to kill a king or a military leader.

Aulos A Greek musical instrument that has a double reed; similar in some respects to a modern oboe.

Barbarians Non-Greeks. In the Greek world all those who were not Greek were called barbarians by the Greeks.

Bireme A ship or galley with two banks or tiers of oars down each side.

Black figured pottery A method of decorating pottery whereby the design was painted in black silhouette over the natural red of the clay.

Capitalist A person who has money or property and uses it to make money in various business enterprises.

Catapult A weapon that operated by the sudden release of tension on wooden beams or twisted cords of horsehair, gut, sinew, or other fiber, and used to hurl stones and other missiles.

Cavalry Those in an army who are mounted on horseback.

Chiton A Greek tunic worn by men and women consisting of two pieces of material pinned or sewn at the shoulders with holes for the arms and head, and gathered at the waist with a girdle. The length of these garments varied.

Choreography The art of composing ballets and other forms of dance and writing the movements down using a special notation.

City-state A political unit of Greece centering on the major cities which were independent of each other and often far apart. The largest city-state was much smaller than the smallest nation. There could be as few as a hundred to as many as a few thousand people living in a city-state.

Coniferous Trees which have spiky needles and produce cones, such as pine, fir, or spruce.

Cuirass A piece of Greek armor covering the chest and back. It was made from linen onto which many bronze scales were attached.

Deciduous Trees and shrubs which lose their leaves each year in winter.

Democracy A form of government or organization where the people contribute to the making of the laws, which they are expected to obey either by electing the people who make the laws, or by being directly involved in the lawmaking process.

Diadems Crowns or headbands adorned with jewels.

Dictatorship A form of government in which one person controls the country usually with armed forces who make sure the dictator's orders are obeyed.

Dowry Money or goods brought to a husband by a wife on marriage.

Drachma A Greek unit of money. One drachma was a standard day's pay in Classical times.

Emmer A hard red wheat with two kernels.

Ephor Overseer; title given to the highest magistrate in Sparta. Time periods were recorded in ancient times by the names of the ephors on a list dating back to 754 B.C.

Epibatai Experienced seamen on Greek warships who were paid for their services.

Equinox Time when the sun crosses the earth's equator making night and day of equal length all over the world. It occurs on about March 21 and September 22 each year.

Evergreen Trees and shrubs which keep their leaves all year.

Foundling An infant found abandoned or a child without a parent or guardian.

Frankincense A highly perfumed gum from trees in the East used to make incense.

Geometry A branch of mathematics which calculates figures in space or the shape of a surface or solid.

Gymnasium High school; place where ancient Greek citizens gathered for education and discussion.

Helots The serfs or slaves of Sparta who were owned by the State and allotted to land-owners to work for them. A proportion of the food they produced went to feed the citizens of Sparta. Helots had no legal rights and were put to death if they tried to escape.

Himation A cloak worn in ancient Greece.

Hoplites Citizen-soldiers of ancient Greece between the ages of eighteen and sixty. They had to pay for their own armor; heavily armed foot soldiers.

Krater Greek vessel usually used for diluting wine with water. It could be made of pottery or metal. Many large expensive kraters were dedicated at temples and used in religious ceremonies.

Lentils Plants which have seeds that are used for food. Their food value is similar to peas and beans.

Medical ethics Rules of proper conduct which should be observed by those practicing medicine.

Mosaic A picture or decoration made of small objects such as stones or glass of different colors. These objects are often set with another substance, such as cement or glue, to fix them in place.

Murals Decorations on or fixed to a wall.

Oikos Name given by the Greeks to the family unit.

Oracles People who were believed to be in direct contact with a god; places where the Greeks believed the gods spoke directly to people.

Panathenaea An elaborate Athenian national festival celebrated every fourth year at high summer; cows and sheep were sacrificed to the goddess Athena.

Papyrus A form of paper made from the fiber of the papyrus reed which grew in eastern countries such as Egypt.

Pebble mosaic A picture decoration made from colored pebbles and fixed in place with glue or cement.

Peplos A woolen robe made from a large single length of cloth and worn by Greek women.

Philosopher One who tries to find explanations and reasons for everything that happens or searches for the truth behind everything.

Quadreme A ship or galley with one bank of oars on each side, rowed by four men pulling the oar in a single wide sweep.

Quinquereme A ship or galley with one bank of oars on each side, rowed by five men pulling the oar in a single wide sweep.

Red figured pottery A method of decorating pottery in which the figures were left in the natural red of the clay and the rest painted black.

Specific gravity A scientific calculation which measures the ratio or relationship between a given amount of a substance and the same amount of a standard substance, such as oil in ratio to water.

Stele An upright stone slab or pillar engraved with an inscription or design and used as a monument or grave marker.

Trigonometry A branch of mathematics which deals with the angles and sides of triangles and is used to calculate distances and heights of things which would otherwise be difficult to measure. Some examples are the heights of mountains or distances through mountain ranges and distances of heavenly bodies.

Trireme A ship or galley with three banks or tiers of oars down each side.

Unireme A ship or galley with one bank of oars on each side.

The Greeks: Some Famous People and Places

HERODOTUS

Herodotus was a Greek historian who was born around 484 B.C. at Halicarnassus. He wrote the first great narrative history of the world. He has been called the "Father of History." Herodotus approached his work in a similar way to that of Hecateus, who recorded and wrote geography. Herodotus also used the methods of those who kept histories of their states. His *History* was of the Greco-Persian Wars.

In piecing together his history, Herodotus was mainly dependent on what he was told, but evaluated this critically. He also traveled and noted what he saw. Very few other Greek or Roman historians were as conscientious in collecting and writing their material as Herodotus was.

ALEXANDER THE GREAT

Alexander the Great is regarded as one of the world's greatest generals. His campaigns included the conquest of Western Asia Minor, the capture of Tyre, Egypt, and Babylon. By 327 B.C. Alexander set out to invade India. He crossed the Indus River in 326 B.C. On his death in 323 B.C. his body was placed in a golden coffin in Alexandria, Egypt, a city that he himself had founded.

ARISTOTLE

Aristotle was a Greek philosopher and scientist who began his studies in the fields of Greek medicine and biology. For three years, he was also a tutor to Alexander the Great. During his early years, Aristotle lived in Pella, the capital of Macedonia. In 335 B.C. he returned to Athens, where he continued his scientific work. He opened the Lyceum, his school of philosophy, where he organized and contributed to its work for the next twelve years. In 323 B.C. he moved to Chalcis, north of Athens, where he died in 322 B.C. Forty-seven of Aristotle's works have survived and these are mainly notes used in his Lyceum courses. The Lyceum lasted for another 250 years after Aristotle.

ARISTARCHUS OF SAMOS

Aristarchus was a Greek astronomer who lived in about 270 B.C. He was the first person to put forward the theory that the earth revolved around the sun. His colleagues at the time thought that he should have been indicted for this outrageous suggestion. His theories were used by Archimedes and Plutarch. The only work of Aristarchus' surviving is the one called *On the Sizes and Distances of the Sun and Moon*.

PYTHAGORAS

The philosopher and mathematician Pythagoras is thought to have lived from 580 to 500 B.C. He migrated to southern Italy in 532 B.C. to escape difficult and harsh political conditions and opened his own academy at Croton in Italy. None of his writings have survived but many mathematical principles and theories are attributed to him, as well as philosophical theories. His teachings influenced Greek and later medieval European thought.

HOMER

Very little is known about Homer's life. It is thought that he lived in Ionia in about 800 to 700 B.C. Two great works, the *Iliad* and the *Odyssey*, have been attributed to Homer. These works have had a great influence, not only on Greek life and thought, but on all Western literature.

STRABO

Much of our knowledge of the ancient world comes from the work of Strabo, a Greek geographer and historian, who was born in about 64 or 63 B.C., and died after A.D. 23. He wrote many works, including *Historical Sketches*, which consisted of forty-seven volumes, written in 20 B.C. Most of this work has been lost. Another of his works, *Geographical Sketches*, describes his geographical principles and the geography of areas of the world including Spain, France, Italy, the Black Sea, Greece, Asia Minor, India, Persia, and the African lands around the Mediterranean.

ATHENS

Athens was the Greek city that has been called the "nursery of Western civilization." It experienced a period of rapid growth in the sixth century B.C. Shrines were replaced with temples. The Temple of Athena was built in about 580 B.C. The Parthenon was later constructed on this site.

In 480 B.C. the city was captured and destroyed by the Persians. In 479 B.C. Athens began to rebuild. Schools such as Plato's Academy and Aristotle's Lyceum were established here.

The Roman general Sulla captured Athens in 86 B.C. Many citizens were killed and a number of public buildings were destroyed, as well as houses. More buildings were added to Athens during the time of the Roman Empire.

SPARTA

Sparta was the ancient capital of the Laconia district. It was a famous military city-state. At the end of the Peloponnesian War in 404 B.C., Sparta was the most powerful state in Greece. In 396 A.D. the city was destroyed by the Visigoths.

MT. OLYMPUS

This is a Greek mountain standing 9,570 feet (2,917 meters) high. It was written about by many writers, including Homer. Mt. Olympus was supposed to be the legendary home of the gods, and the site of the Throne of Zeus.

Index